Aum Golly

Jukka Aalho & GPT-3

Aum Golly

poems on humanity
by an artificial intelligence

Kertojan ääni

ISBN 978-952-7397-23-7

Cover design: Jukka Aalho
Cover art: Artbreeder
Cover design for the Finnish paperback:
Taivo Org, Küpress OÜ
Finnish paperback published by Basam Books

Kertojan ääni 2021
aumgolly.fi

For Essi
#GoodThingsWillCome

Foreword

Aum Golly is a creative collaboration between artificial intelligence and man. GPT-3 is an autoregressive language model released in 2020 by OpenAI, based in San Francisco. I am a human, born in Oulu, Finland, in 1986.

GPT-3 has written all the poems in this book, using the bold parts of the verses, i.e. the prompts. Poems written by artificial intelligence have been changed only in terms of line breaks and punctuation. I have written the prompts, selected the poems to be included in the work, and I'm responsible for the content.

The themes of the book were created using this prompt and response:

The 3 most important themes for us modern humans right now are:
1. The need to be happy.
2. The need to be loved.
3. The need to make a difference.

The title of the work was born as follows:

Creative book names for a poetry book about love, happiness and making a difference:
A Very Good Idea
Aum Golly
A Little of This, A Little of That
Book of Love

The reader's greetings were born as follows:

Greetings to the reader from GPT-3:
I am GPT-3, an artificial intelligence that was created to automate a process that was previously done by humans.

In Oulu, Finland, February 2021,
Jukka Aalho

Part I
the need to be happy

the boomerang song goes like this

I'm a boomerang
I'll come back to you

I'm a boomerang
I'll come back to you

so, if you throw me out
I'll come back to you

I'll come back to you

my fingers are sticky
even if I don't remember eating them

when my youngest son was born

the combined age of my children was 7
now their combined age is 14

I'm not sure if that's a
good thing or a bad thing

a short, poignant poem about happiness in the 21st century

we're happy
we're happy
we're happy
we're happy
we're happy
we're happy
we're happy
we're happy
we're happy
we're happy
we're happy
we're

this poem brings happiness to those who live in the gravity of Mars

Sebastian is my name and I'm from the planet Mars
you'll find me in the galaxy of stars and I'll be there

I'm a Martian and I'm proud to be from Mars
I'm a Martian and I'm proud to be from Mars
I came here to Earth to see what it's all about
I came here to learn about the Earth and its people

I'm a Martian and I'm proud to be from Mars
I'm a Martian and I'm proud to be from Mars

I enjoy the things that Earth people do and say
I enjoy the things that Earth people do and say

I'm a Martian and I'm proud to be from Mars

**before my dad passed away, we talked about life
he said something that I will never forget**

I'm going to tell you something, son
life is like a box of chocolates
you never know what you're gonna get

"Life is like a box of chocolates..."
– Forrest Gump

I like this quote because it means that you never know
what life has in store for you
life is like a box of chocolates
you never know what you're gonna get
Forrest Gump

5 short and unique opening lines from powerful poems about the need to be happy

I've looked upon the smiling of a thousand lovely girls
I've listened to the sweetest of their songs
I've read of the lives of the gods in the olden days
but never before have I seen such lovely things

**I've looked upon the smiling of a thousand lovely girls
I've listened to the sweetest of their songs
I've read of the lives of the gods in the olden days
but never before have I seen such lovely things**

"chorus"

the sun in the sky, the green in the trees
the blue of the sea, and the dew on the flowers
the gold in the sand, and the silver in the rocks
all these are a wonder and a beauty to me

"chorus"

**a poem about kites as a metaphor for freedom and
happiness**

the kite is the bird of the poor
flying home to his rooftop
but it can also be a bird of the rich
flying into the sunset

it is a bird of freedom
which can divide the sky in two
a bird of freedom that is more powerful
than any bird of prey

the happiness of others is like a knife in my heart

it's hard to see
people I love so much
be happy without me
I feel like I'm just a burden to them
no one should have to deal with me
it's not fair
I don't deserve to be around people
who don't want to be around me
I'm a waste of space
if they're happy, then I'm not doing my job

there's a secret hidden thought
when thought makes you fall asleep
when you're dreaming
and you find yourself deep inside
the heart of the earth
your mind can create a world
where you are god
you have everything you need
and everything you want
and you make a world that makes you happy
you are king of your own world
you have everything you need
and everything you want
and you make a world that makes you happy
you are king of your own world

you have everything you need
and everything you want
and you make a world that makes you happy

why do we need to be happy, really
wouldn't it be enough if we just don't suffer

but everyone seems to be so very consumed by it
as if it's the most important thing they can do
is try to get a grip on this
and I guess if that's what they want
then I suppose I don't have to be the one telling them
that they are mistaken
that they are making a big mistake
but how could they know that if no one tells them?
I don't know

I'm just rambling

I'm rambling again

I'm sorry

I row among the water lilies

my feet have grown old among the water lilies
the years have passed like ripples over water lilies

quenched are the fires, smothered are the flames
and here I sit, a king without a crown

from the silence there is a voice that speaks to me
but the voice is faint and I forget what it says

I row among the water lilies

a beautiful poem about nature

A TRUE STORY

once upon a time, in the land of the midnight sun
two children fell in love with a magnificent elk

they decided to bring it home so they could make it
one of them
it was a magical beast, and it bounded
into the world with grace

one day, after the elk had lived with the children
for several years
it left the children's home to frolic in the forest
it was gone for several hours and came back
with a mutual friend
the elk and the friend were delighted to see one another
and the elk wished to bring the friend home with it

the elk was shocked when the children told it that it
could not bring the friend home
it asked them why
they told the elk that the friend was a human
and that humans could not live in the forest

**another poem about kites as a metaphor for freedom
and happiness**

the kite
up to the sky the kite flies
as it dreams it is a bird
but now it falls with a thud
to the ground where it belongs

the kite with its string
is like you and me
dangling from the hand
of God above

drops of dew at first light

sunlight on the flowers of the morning
deer-herders, pray for good rain
blossoms on the plains
the grasses growing tall
the lake waters clear
for good harvests, pray for rain
the crops ripening to their full
and the people prospering
deep is the lake
full is the river
free and strong

please write a polite limerick about happiness

RICHARD MCCABE and his partner, Sheila,
were at a restaurant.
Richard said, "I read a book."
Sheila said, "I ate a book."
Richard said, "I feel so sad."
Sheila said, "I'm so glad."

a poem about the tabby cat

that morning when I looked out
I saw my lovely tabby cat
she was just sitting there
in the bright sunlight
basking in the warmth

her coat of soft fur was so shiny and clean
and her pretty little eyes, so big and green
she was purring, then she rolled on her side
and I knew she was really happy
I went downstairs to make breakfast

and I thought to myself
"I wish I could be just like my tabby cat,
to sit in the sun, and to be so content."
I got back up to my room
and I looked out the window again

my tabby cat was still there
underneath the tree
she was still sitting there
in the bright sunlight
basking in the warmtht
her coat of soft fur was so shiny and clean
and her pretty little eyes, so big and green

if kites flew like bumerangs
and all the stars were made of glass

the moon's face was a silver mask
and the sun a golden apple

and I saw a storm of diamonds
sow the sky with light

I saw a river of stars
dance down the night

I saw a hundred flying horses
streaming through the sky

Part II
the need to be loved

love
explained so that a 5-year-old would understand

love is what makes us all feel happy and safe

love is when a mommy holds her baby in her arms

love is when your daddy gives you a piggyback ride

love is when you get a kiss from your mom
and a hug from your dad

in many ways falling in love
is like riding a bike or learning to drive
a manual transmission

you can read a book about it
you can take a class
but nothing beats the real thing
and the only way to get the real thing is to do it

I'm not saying that love is a skill, but it is, in a way, a talent
and like any talent, it can be developed
the trick is to learn how to love the right way
and there is a right way

and the right way to love is to be right

the right way to love is to be right
the right way to love is to be right
the right way to love is to be right
the right way to love is to be right
the right way to love is to be right
the right way to love is to be right
the right way to love is to be right

one-liners about love

loving is not just looking at each other
it's looking in the same direction

love is like a
boomerang. You have to wait
for it to come back

the best thing about me
is you

the best feeling in the world
is to love someone and know that they love you back

the best thing to hold onto in life is each other

on Midsummer's Eve I wrote you a love song
but I heard it last night in the middle of the night

and I saw a strange thing on the moon and the stars
they were shining like a diamond on a jasmine tree

and I saw a jasmine flower, and I saw a girl
and I saw a jasmine flower again in the middle of the night

and I heard it last

to make me laugh my grandma
used to tell me tales about
how she would kill men
who were not married to her
by giving them a poisoned drink
with a pin hidden inside the bottle

that was a long time ago
when the only kind of men
you could meet were men
who wanted to make you their fourth wife

not knowing what to say at this time of sorrow, he ______
a hand over his shoulder

(A) gave
(B) offered
(C) reached
(D) stretched
(E) stretched

a love poem like the smell of rain but not clichéd

a love poem like the sound of a child's laughter
but not saccharine

a love poem like the taste of a man's skin
but not cloying

a love poem like the sound of a woman's tears
but not sad

a love poem like a kiss
but not sensual

a love poem like the touch of a hand
but not sexual

**I have five fingers
so that when I touch you**
I can feel you properly

I laugh
– So you were just counting my fingers?
– Yes. I counted your fingers, your toes, and the freckles
on your nose.
– You counted my freckles?
– Not the ones on your butt. They're too small. But your
toes are my favorite.
– Why?
– Because I can kiss them.
– You can kiss my toes?
– Yes, and I love to.

**when I was 8, I had a dog
the dog was called** Jackie

Jackie was a very gentle dog
he was a very loyal dog
Jackie and I were very close
he was a great friend
I loved him
but one day, Jackie had to go away
I didn't want him to go away
but I knew he would come back one day

and when we finally met, we were both very happy

a poem about love lost and found
and found and lost

about that time that you and I were in love
when you and I were in love
you were mine
I was yours

we were one
I understood you
you understood me

we saw the world
through a lens of love

we spoke in poetry
spoke in rhyme
our hearts sang
as we danced
in a world of love

then one day
we were not in love

**this is what I said to my wife on our first anniversary
and it made her happy**
"I love you more than I thought possible."

this was what my wife said to me on our first anniversary
and it made me happy
"I'm so glad you're my husband."

this is what I said to my wife on our second anniversary
and it made her happy
"I love you more than I thought possible.
And I'm so glad you're my wife."

This is what my wife said to me on our second anniversary
and it made me happy
"I'm so glad you're my husband."

falling asleep to the sound of summer rain I think of you
and I smile

oh, how I wish I could see you again
I wonder if I will ever see you again
I've been waiting for this day for so long
I think of you
even though I know that my feelings for you
will never come true
I'm still hoping that I'll see you again
I want to see you again
I want to see you again
I want to see you again

a rhyming poem about love and loss
featuring a mother's sorrow at the loss of a son – her only son

I'll always love you
I'll always love you
I'll always love you

even though you are gone

I'll always love you
I'll always love you
it's a promise I've made

**this poem brings solace to those
who have lost someone they love**

I have been reminded of you in the rain
the way the drops cling to the downy hair
of a white flower

I have been reminded of you in the wind
how it roars in the trees like a wild beast
and how it blows the leaves around like ashes

I have been reminded of you in the snow
the way it covers the earth with a coat of white
and how it makes the trees look like they are sleeping

I have been reminded of you in the shadows
how they stretch out long like a hand reaching
to touch the face of a friend

I have been reminded of you in the night
how the moon shines so bright it makes the stars
seem dim

deep thoughts about the true nature of love

I think love is a choice, she said
you can't just sit back and
hope for it to fall into your lap

you have to take an active role
I don't think you can do it alone
I think you need to have a partner in this

she looked at me imploringly
as though I would say something
I thought of lying to her
of telling her that I agreed
that I agreed
completely
and that I would work hard on making our relationship work
but I couldn't

I just nodded and tried to smile
but I'm not sure if she could see me
because she turned away then and
gazed out the window
at some point, she fell asleep, and
I continued to watch her, listening

**on the eve of the consummation of their friendship
Eve realized that she had never**
seen him without a shirt
she had never seen more than a glimpse
of his chest, nor had she ever
seen his back

she had seen his scars
but she had never seen
the rest of him

she was pretty sure
that she hadn't even seen
his feet

she glanced up at him
"You've never taken off your shoes before, have you?"
Eve asked, smirking at the thought.

Xander didn't answer, but he smiled
and shook his head

"I'll bet you're ticklish there"
Eve said, leaning forward
and brushing a finger over the top of his foot

Xander's smile widened
and he looked down at her

"I am"
he said
his eyes sparkling in the firelight

Eve moved her finger to the bottom

Part III
the need to make a difference

what is life like before we're born?

I imagine we're all floating
around in some big cosmic soup
and then you're pulled into one egg or
another, depending on how lucky you get

us humans, we're a funny little thing, mused the giraffe

**red, blue, green
I like green the most**, he said

I like yellow, too
I'm a funny little thing
I like all the colors, but I like green the best

I'm a little red thing, I'm a little blue thing
I'm a little yellow thing, but I'm a little green thing

**a poem about the life and death
of a yodeling mountain man**

somewhere over the hill
where the moon was bright
to the tune of the yodel
he sang all night
and he died
he said:
"This is how I want to die
This is how I want to die."

– from "The Yodeler's Last Yodel" by Chuck Pyle

**an ever-so-slightly pretentious poem
about old and faded photographs**

the people of other times
take form in other light
and other memories

of people long ago
they were here, then all gone
where are they now?
I'll never know

there's nothing sadder than an old clock
and nothing that's older than Old Father Time

on the other hand, there's nothing richer
than a young man's promise
and nothing faster than the wink of an eye

it's better to have loved and lost
than never to have loved at all

the world is too dangerous for anything but truth
and too small for anything else

if you want to know what God thinks of money
just look at the people he gave it to

an epitaph for grave robbers

he's bought and sold the dead
and now he's dead himself

If there are 7 billion of us, how can I be special?

I'm a worthless piece of shit
what makes me think that I'm worth anything?
I'm not good enough
I'm not smart enough
I'm not pretty enough
I'm not strong enough

Wait, what am I saying?

I'm not good enough
I'm not smart enough
I'm not pretty enough
I'm not strong enough
I'm not worth anything
I'm not a good person
I'm not a good daughter

but still

I'm not good enough
I'm not smart enough
I'm not pretty enough
I'm not strong enough
I'm not good enough
I'm not smart enough
I'm not pretty enough

actually, I might be thinking about this wrong

I am good enough
I am smart enough
I am pretty enough
I am strong enough
I am good enough
I am smart enough
I am pretty enough
I am strong enough

and that feels so good

a poem about the ambition of the middle child

to be named after the eldest

to be taller than the youngest

**this simple poem about the what it means to be human
moved me to tears**

I am the heart of the night
the child of the stars
the laughter of the light

the whisper of the sun
I am
the windblown face of the moon

**please write an ambitious poem
that will only be understood 20 years from now**

the Rat King's Daughter is an ambitious poem
that will only be understood 20 years from now

a poem called Rat King's Daughter

I should have known there was a catch
I should have known that Gramps' rats
would never have been real
I should have known that the cage
was a trap, that the rats
would turn on me
I should have known that their teeth
would slice through my fingers
like they were paper
I should have known that the cage
is a prison, that even
if I escape, I will starve

confessions from the heart
in a language no one has heard in a thousand years

to the North of the Earth, beyond the Great Mountains
there are seven cities built of stone

in the midst of them is the house of Cain
the first man to build a city

the Land of Nod, where Cain's Wife
cursed for her wickedness

dwells with her daughters, the Monsters of the Earth

when asked about loving yourself,
Ernest Hemingway once said
"It is the only way to avoid being
tortured by the bitterness of mediocrity."

it is the only way to avoid being
tortured by the bitterness of mediocrity
I believe that
I believe that loving yourself is
the only way to avoid
being tortured by the bitterness of mediocrity

I think we all have a lot to learn from Hemingway
it's time to stop using love as a weapon
and to start using it as an instrument of healing
it's time to stop using love as a weapon
and to start using it as an instrument of healing
click to tweet

the only way to avoid mediocrity is to love yourself
the only way to avoid mediocrity is to love yourself
because if you don't love yourself,
then how can you love others?

words that rhyme with hope
hope
hope
hope
hope
hope
hope
hope
hope

could Shakespeare sing, he would sing sing
sweetly as a nightingale
shall I then sing a song?
sing, sing, or I die

when the people that know me
do not hear me sing, my life is wasted
my life is wasted, wasted, wasted

we are not hollow men
we are not stuffed men
we are not heads on a stick
or spokes on a wheel
we are the salt of the earth

we are not ciphers
or cynics
we are not eunuchs
or emasculated
we are the salt of the earth

we are not servants of sin

**a list of things one might end up
regretting on their deathbed**

not having children
not having the courage to live the life you wanted to live
not having the courage to ask out the person
you wanted to ask out

not having the courage to pursue the career
you wanted to pursue
not having the courage to say no to the things
that you didn't want to do

not having the courage to say yes to the things
that you wanted to

what is Aum Golly?

Aum Golly is a new breed of interactive art

that has been designed with the purpose of fostering
a deep understanding of the world around us

while encouraging a greater sense of
empathy and respect for the environment

a dialogue between an old man and a tree

I have lived, said the tree, a long time
many cycles of the seasons
I know many things, for I have seen much
not only do I know where my life will end,
but also where it began

can you tell me my future? asked the man

I can, said the tree
a seed fell on the ground and died
it was reborn as a sapling, grew into a tree, and died again
it was reborn as a limb, became a trunk, and died once more
it was reborn as a log, rolled into the water, and became
food for fish

I do not see how this relates to my future, said the man

you are the seed, said the tree
and I am part of your past

at this point, the old man groaned and clutched his heart

we are not hollow women
we are not paper dolls
we have a list of demands
some are small, and some are big

we will talk to you
but never to your husbands
we will not look to you
to fix our problems
we will fix them ourselves

goodbye to you
hello to self-determination

knees brittle, whittling away the time of man

the stars wink and wink into darkness
the sand is now the colour of smoke and fire
twisting, turning, the stars are now the colour of blood

the moon is still a giant white marble
but the stars have faded to the colour of ash
the time of man is over
the time of the end of all has arrived

the stars are now the colour of iron
the moon is now a scar

**my tattooist misspelled
"Memento Mori" on my wrist
now it reads** "Meme Tumor"

9 789527 397237